FUN ROOMS

Home Theaters, Music Studios, Game Rooms, and more

FUN ROOMS

Home Theaters, Music Studios, Game Rooms, and more

COLLINS | DESIGN

An Imprint of HarperCollinsPublishers

FUN ROOMS: HOME THEATERS, MUSIC STUDIOS, GAME ROOMS, AND MORE
Copyright © 2005 by COLLINS DESIGN and LOFT Publications

HarperCollins books may be purchased for educational, business, or sales promotional use.
For information, please write: Special Markets Department, HarperCollins Publishers Inc.,
10 East 53rd Street, New York, NY 10022

First Edition published in 2005 by:
Collins Design
An Imprint of HarperCollins*Publishers*
10 East 53rd Street
New York, NY 10022
Tel.: (212) 207-7000
Fax: (212) 207-7654
CollinsDesign@harpercollins.com
www.harpercollins.com

Distributed throughout the world by:
HarperCollins*Publishers*
10 East 53rd Street
New York, NY 10022
Fax: (212) 207-7654

Packaged by
LOFT Publications
Via Laietana 32, 4° Of. 92
08003 Barcelona, Spain
Tel.: +34 932 688 088
Fax: +34 932 687 073
loft@loftpublications.com
www.loftpublications.com

Editor:
Ana G. Cañizares

Art Director:
Mireia Casanovas Soley

Layout:
Ignasi Gracia Blanco

Library of Congress Cataloging-in-Publication Data

Cañizares, Ana Cristina G.
  Fun Rooms: home theaters, music studios, game rooms, and more / Ana G. Canizares.-- 1st ed.
     p. cm.
  ISBN 0-06-082991-5 (hardcover)
  1. Recreation rooms. 2. Interior decoration. I. Title.
  NK2117.R4C36 2005
  747.7'91--dc22
                                    2005021799

Printed by: Anman Gràfiques del Vallès
Spain

D.L: B-35.966-2005

First Printing, 2005

SUMMARY

FUN ROOMS

Nobody would question the right for any child to have his or her own playroom. But what about adults? Perhaps it is not so much that we are entitled to it as we are in dire need of it. Today's stressful lifestyle and hectic surroundings take their toll on both body and mind, and sometimes all we feel like doing is retreating into the comfort of our own home to relax and escape from the responsibilities of adult life. In other words, we want to feel like a kid again. This book explores the idea of playrooms inside the home, especially those geared to adults, but also those that can be enjoyed by children as well. From high-tech gadgets and state-of-the-art equipment to table games and funky furniture, the selection of interiors and elements presented in this *Fun Rooms* collection can serve as an inspiration to those looking to create their own fun room at home or simply offer a glimpse into the realm of home entertainment design.

Lights Out
This chapter switches off the lights to welcome spaces devoted to visual entertainment—namely, home cinemas—and nocturnal events such as parties and gatherings. Possibly the most popular type of entertainment room, it is no wonder that home cinemas comprise the greater part of the fun rooms presented in this book. No longer the preserve of the rich and famous, home cinemas are now accessible to a wider public, thanks to advances in technology and a broad range of high-quality products. LCD (liquid crystal display) screens, plasma screens, projection televisions, and projectors, in combination with top-notch audio systems, can make for an authentic home theater environment. Choosing the right furnishings, colors, textures, and materials can also be crucial to achieving an attractive atmosphere with optimal viewing conditions. In the case of living rooms with bar areas, these can also be transformed into fun rooms through imaginative designs and stylistic details.

Time-Out

For those who need a pause from their automatic mode, fun rooms can function as a place in which to unwind, by either simply relaxing or seeking distraction through active play. This chapter features a variety of spaces, including indoor pools, billiard rooms, game rooms, and children's playrooms. These fun rooms can be as elaborate or as minimalist as taste allows; the importance lies in creating a stylish environment where diversion comes first.

Play It by Ear

Whether it be a professional music studio, piano room, or living area with a fully equipped sound system, this section explores rooms used for playing instruments or listening to music. Our sense of hearing can be indulged by the very best in audio equipment and complemented by a visually aesthetic design to ensure a comfortable and pleasant listening experience.

FUNiture & Things

Furniture itself can create a fun environment through the use of color, texture, and form. Casual elements such as poufs and pillows generate a laid-back attitude reminiscent of childhood settings, while the mixture of retro and contemporary styles adds a lively and carefree quality to any space. New trends in interior design, led by young and innovative designers, now provide us with playful accessories and a broad range of equipment that not only improve the quality of our fun rooms, but also give them an attractive appearance in order to integrate them into any given space.

Lights Out

Hit the lights and watch the action: Home cinemas, bars, and party spaces

Sebastià Garcia House

Installation: **Werner**

Location: **Barcelona, Spain**

Photos © **Gogortza/Llorella**

An exotic interior design characterized by Asian references, intense colors, and abstract paintings creates a sensuous and lively ambience fit for hosting gatherings, parties, and private screenings. A high-definition projector, sound system, and screen allow for an integral viewing experience, while an exuberantly decorated bar provides an animated atmosphere for parties and get-togethers.

Bachelor Pad

Design: **Cortney and Robert Novogratz**
Location: **New York, NY, USA**
Photos © **Joshua McHugh**

Previously an old gun shop, this space in Manhattan's Soho district was converted into a slick bachelor pad for an affluent client who desired a house specially equipped for parties and gatherings. The barroom enjoys a generous space equipped with a U-shaped bar built on-site out of mahogany and topped with a zinc counter fabricated in France. Fitted with its own fireplace and leather armchairs, the room accommodates a large number of people and seats at least 10 at the bar. The space is animated by bright-colored walls, lively paintings, and vintage posters and signs. The wine cellar features wine racks from Italy, a butcher's table from Hungary, and small stools from a school in France.

Wine-Tasting Room

Design: **Lundberg Design**
Location: **Napa, CA, USA**
Photos © **Cesar Rubio**

During the process of converting what was formerly a dilapidated barn into a modern residence, the architects of the project discovered a hidden storage space accessed through a floor hatch. In response to the client's request, the space was transformed into an intimate wine-tasting room and cellar with a new glass portal-like entry. While preserving the exposed concrete, stone, and exposed-wood ceilings, the architects invigorated the room with a bold red color, red floor cushions, wine racks, and a tasting table.

Cinema Lounge

Design: **Jo Warman**
Location: **London, UK**
Photos © **Mike Daines/Redcover.com**

This chill-out lounge was specifically designed to seat many people for relaxing movie sessions. Characterized by a stretch of low lounge seating, the space is dominated by a panoramic plasma screen and a curved central table with an integrated open fireplace. The contemporary furnishings, white walls, colored lighting, and overall minimalist design create a cool, laid-back atmosphere fit for late-night flicks and sophisticated parties.

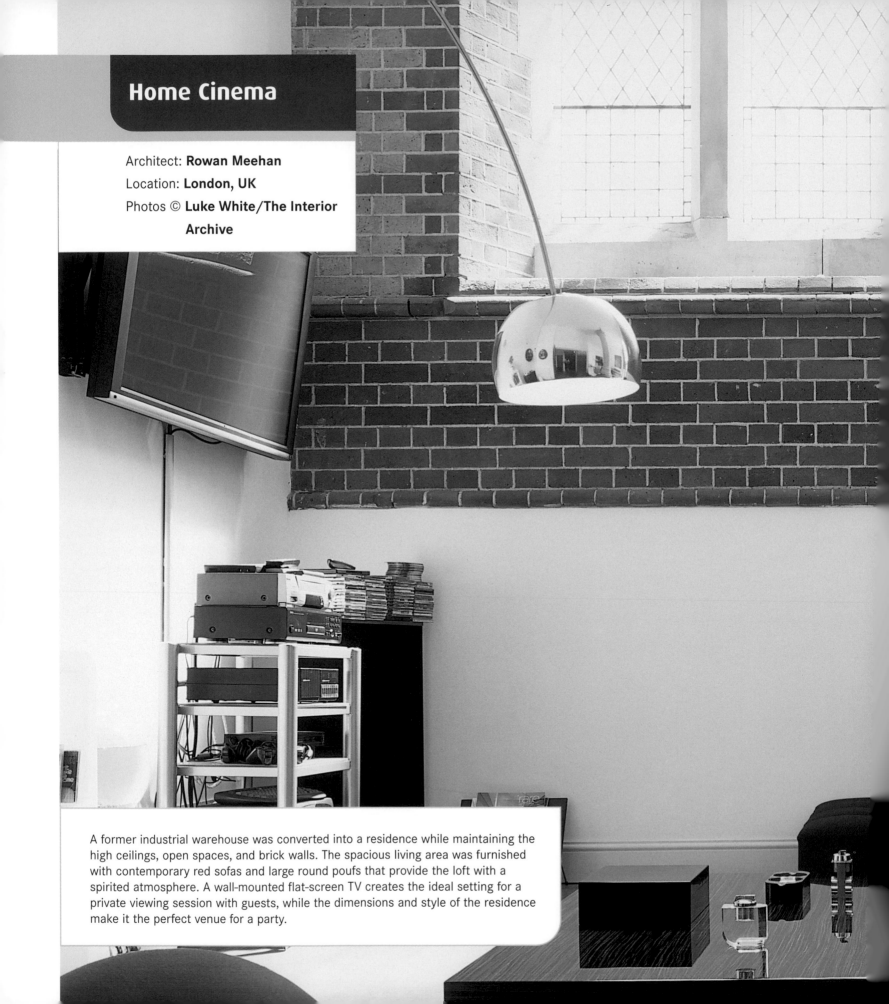

Home Cinema

Architect: **Rowan Meehan**
Location: **London, UK**
Photos © **Luke White/The Interior Archive**

A former industrial warehouse was converted into a residence while maintaining the high ceilings, open spaces, and brick walls. The spacious living area was furnished with contemporary red sofas and large round poufs that provide the loft with a spirited atmosphere. A wall-mounted flat-screen TV creates the ideal setting for a private viewing session with guests, while the dimensions and style of the residence make it the perfect venue for a party.

Q-Loft

Design: **Resolution: 4 Architecture**
Location: **New York, NY, USA**
Photos © **Floto + Warner**

Created for the editor in chief of Marvel Comics in New York, this loft was designed to accommodate not only a pleasant living space with spectacular views of the Empire State Building, but also an entertainment space in which the owner could enjoy the pleasures of a home theater. The theater, featuring a large screen concealed behind wooden panels, can be joined with the remaining areas of the loft through sliding partitions.

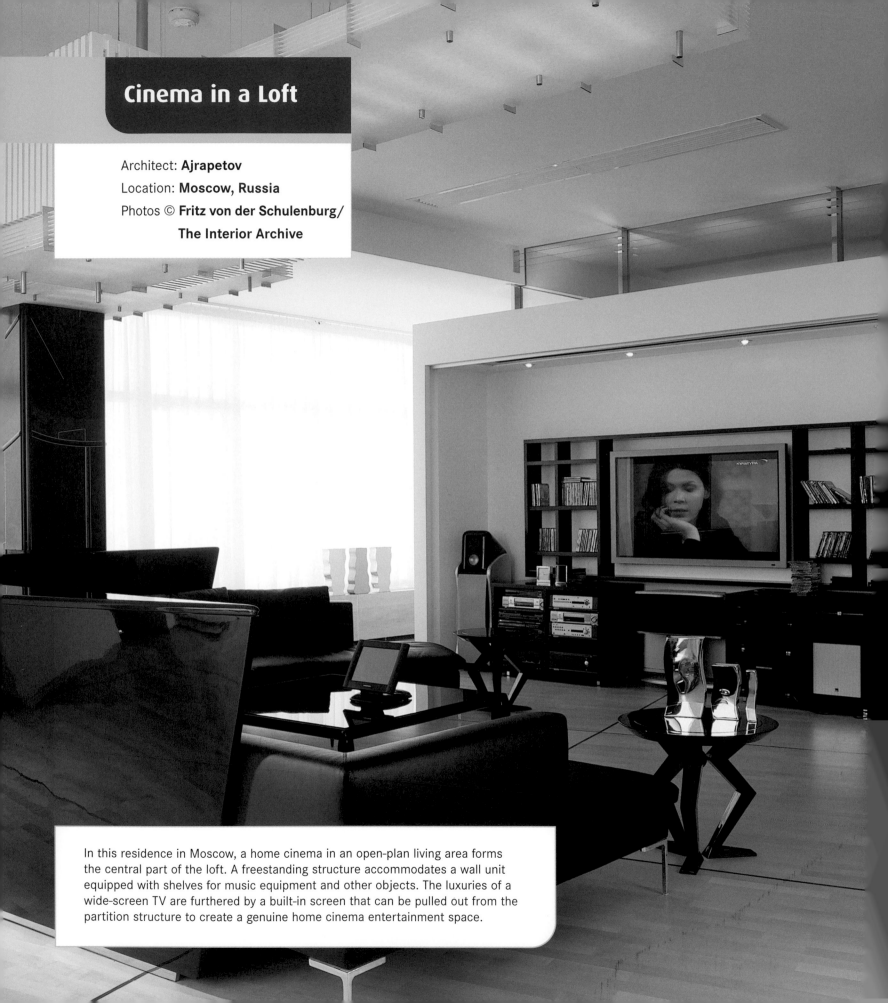

Cinema in a Loft

Architect: **Ajrapetov**

Location: **Moscow, Russia**

Photos © **Fritz von der Schulenburg/ The Interior Archive**

In this residence in Moscow, a home cinema in an open-plan living area forms the central part of the loft. A freestanding structure accommodates a wall unit equipped with shelves for music equipment and other objects. The luxuries of a wide-screen TV are furthered by a built-in screen that can be pulled out from the partition structure to create a genuine home cinema entertainment space.

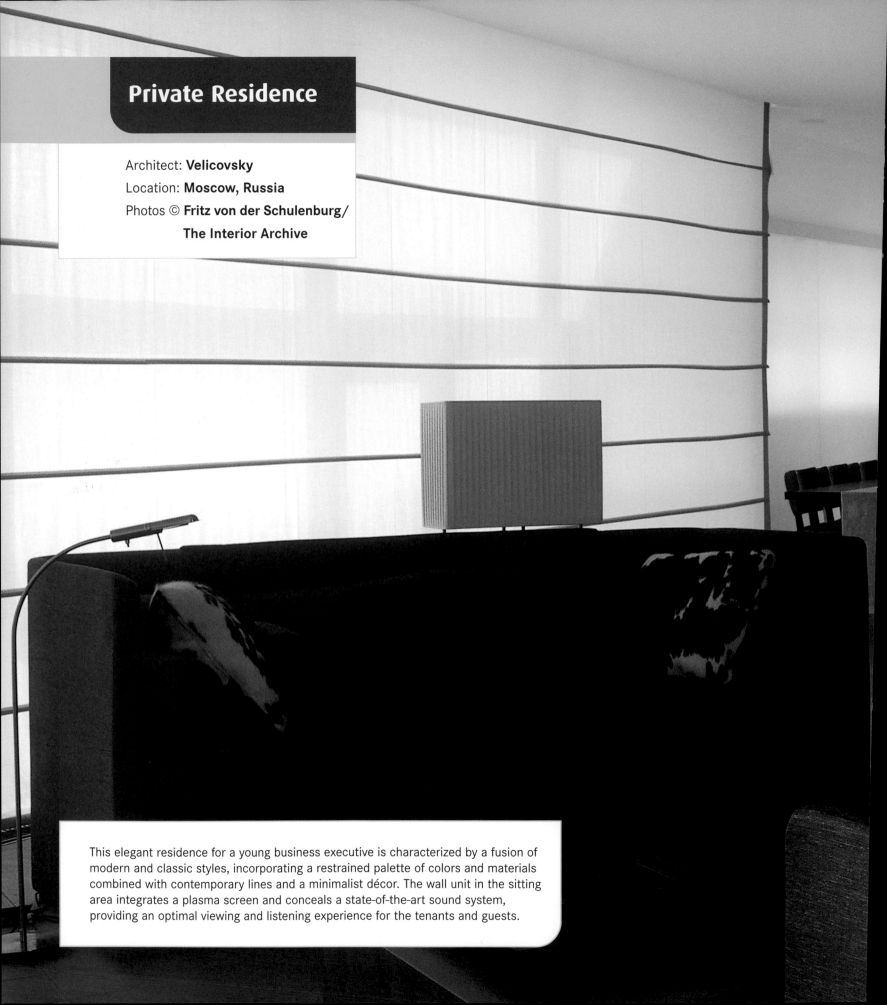

Private Residence

Architect: **Velicovsky**

Location: **Moscow, Russia**

Photos © **Fritz von der Schulenburg/ The Interior Archive**

This elegant residence for a young business executive is characterized by a fusion of modern and classic styles, incorporating a restrained palette of colors and materials combined with contemporary lines and a minimalist décor. The wall unit in the sitting area integrates a plasma screen and conceals a state-of-the-art sound system, providing an optimal viewing and listening experience for the tenants and guests.

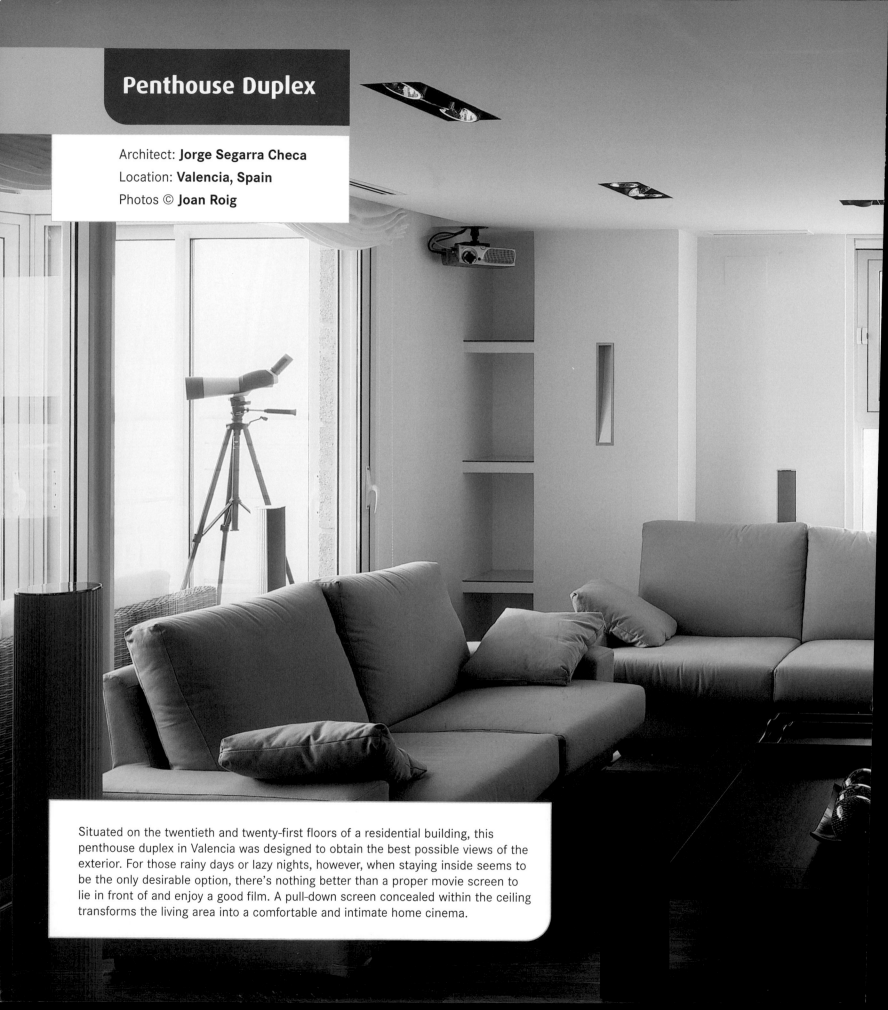

Penthouse Duplex

Architect: **Jorge Segarra Checa**
Location: **Valencia, Spain**
Photos © **Joan Roig**

Situated on the twentieth and twenty-first floors of a residential building, this penthouse duplex in Valencia was designed to obtain the best possible views of the exterior. For those rainy days or lazy nights, however, when staying inside seems to be the only desirable option, there's nothing better than a proper movie screen to lie in front of and enjoy a good film. A pull-down screen concealed within the ceiling transforms the living area into a comfortable and intimate home cinema.

Loft Lopez

Architect: **Lopez Rivera Arquitectes**
Location: **Barcelona, Spain**
Photos © **Jordi Miralles**

This two-story loft was endowed with a large projection screen situated above a shelf unit in the living area. The strategic placement of the screen allows the projected images to be viewed either from the living room or from an exterior terrace on the upper level. The installation provides the opportunity for outdoor viewing sessions during the warmer months and creates an ideal environment for house parties.

Jordi Sarabia House

Installation: **Pont Reyes**
Location: **Barcelona, Spain**
Photos © **Gogortza/Llorella**

The full-height mural flanking the stairway that leads to this sophisticated home cinema already hints at the owner's passion for fantasy and film. Beyond a glass wall, an oversized sofa looks onto a wall unit that houses sound equipment, a flat-screen TV, and a pull-down projection screen. The wall behind displays a large mural of a DreamWorks film poster, and in an adjacent room, a home gym is equipped with large speakers for listening to music while exercising.

House in Rome

Architect: **Patrizio Romano Paris**

Location: **Rome, Italy**

Photos © **Reto Guntli/Zapaimages**

The designer took advantage of the high ceilings of this house in Rome by introducing a mezzanine level that accommodates a viewing area with authentic cinema seating. The balcony looks onto the living area on the main level of the residence, and was designed as a place from which to view films projected onto a screen that pulls down from a recessed slot in the ceiling. The plush chairs and wooden-beam ceiling overhead create an intimate atmosphere for a genuine cinematic experience.

Loft in New York

Architect: **Roger Hirsch, Myriam Corti + Tocar Inc.**
Location: **New York, NY, USA**
Photos © **Michael Moran**

In order to obtain a diaphanous open space, partitions were removed during the renovation of this New York loft. The living area, which features a long shelf unit that functions as a working area when open, was equipped with a movie projector that makes use of the white wall above to allow the tenants and guests to enjoy a quality viewing experience with minimum effort.

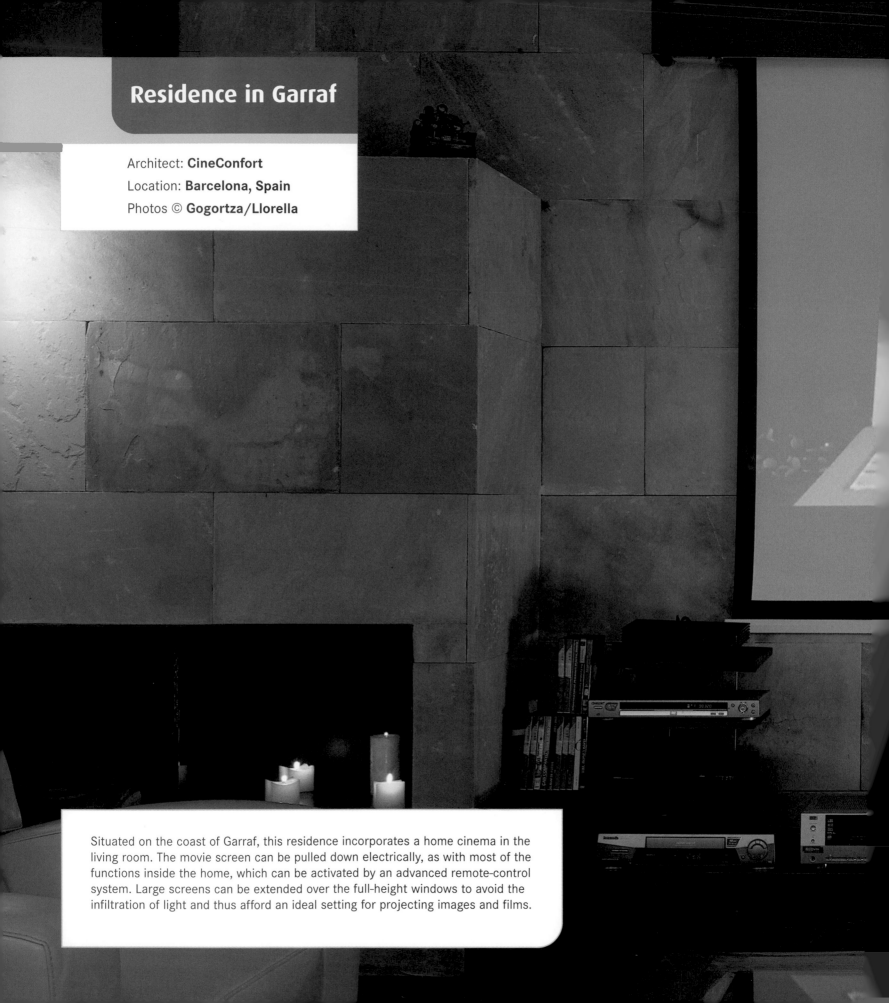

Residence in Garraf

Architect: **CineConfort**
Location: **Barcelona, Spain**
Photos © **Gogortza/Llorella**

Situated on the coast of Garraf, this residence incorporates a home cinema in the living room. The movie screen can be pulled down electrically, as with most of the functions inside the home, which can be activated by an advanced remote-control system. Large screens can be extended over the full-height windows to avoid the infiltration of light and thus afford an ideal setting for projecting images and films.

VXO House

Architect: **Alison Brooks Architects**
Location: **London, UK**
Photos © **Dennis Gilbert/VIEW**

Through the creation of three individual structures, the VXO project aims to integrate landscape, structural form, and site-specific art into a visual and spatial narrative. The V-House, which contains the main living spaces, features a comfortable family room in which to enjoy movies at home. A screen rolled up within an apparatus situated below the ceiling can be pulled down to transform the living area into a home cinema.

Oriol Serra Residence

Installation: **Werner**
Location: **Barcelona, Spain**
Photos © **Gogortza/Llorella**

This triplex loft belonging to a young bachelor incorporates a home cinema, piano room, and bar distributed over the various levels of the residence. A screen can be pulled down in front of the living area's double-height windows to hold a movie session, while the high-definition projector, professional speakers, and amplifiers guarantee high-quality images and sound. Downstairs, a small corner was transformed into a bar, making room for a wine rack underneath the staircase.

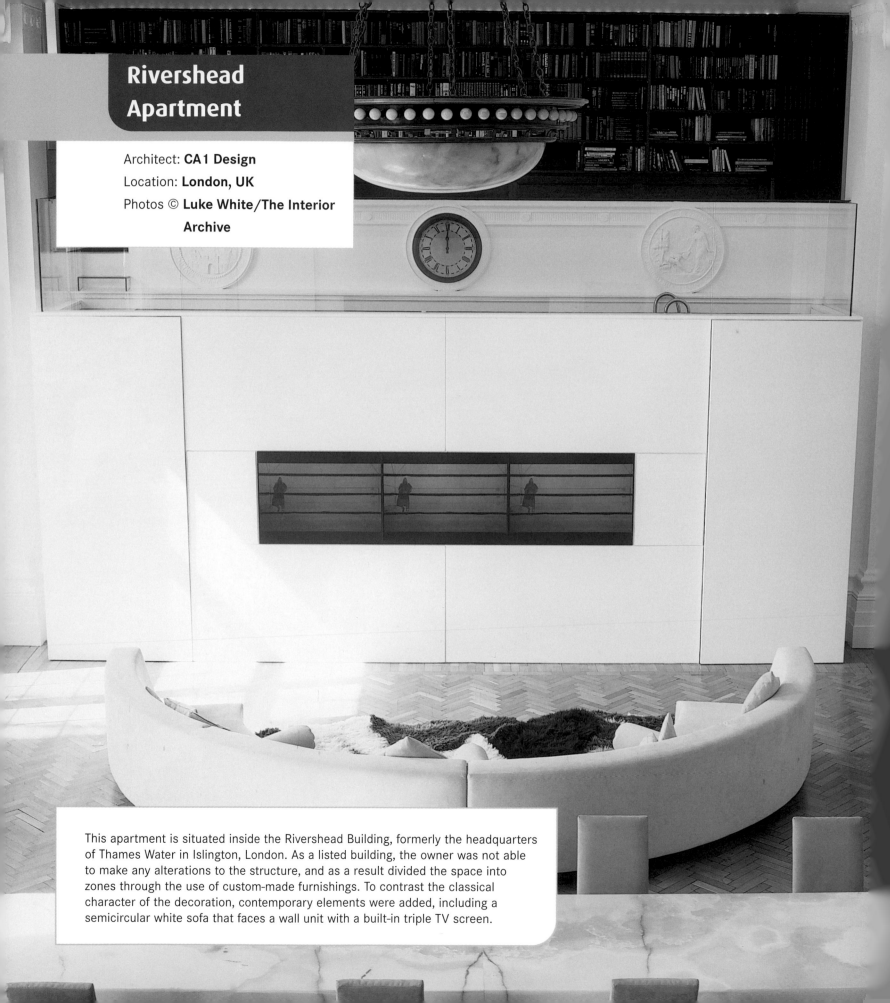

Rivershead Apartment

Architect: **CA1 Design**

Location: **London, UK**

Photos © **Luke White/The Interior Archive**

This apartment is situated inside the Rivershead Building, formerly the headquarters of Thames Water in Islington, London. As a listed building, the owner was not able to make any alterations to the structure, and as a result divided the space into zones through the use of custom-made furnishings. To contrast the classical character of the decoration, contemporary elements were added, including a semicircular white sofa that faces a wall unit with a built-in triple TV screen.

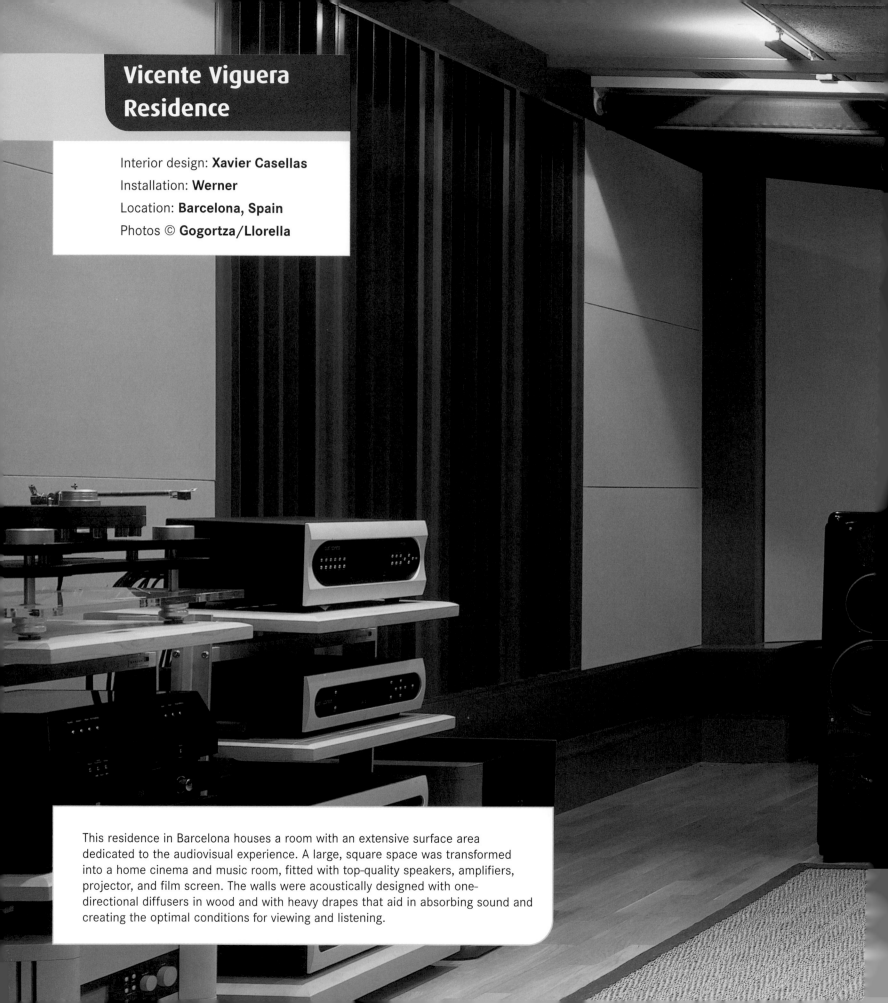

Vicente Viguera Residence

Interior design: **Xavier Casellas**
Installation: **Werner**
Location: **Barcelona, Spain**
Photos © **Gogortza/Llorella**

This residence in Barcelona houses a room with an extensive surface area dedicated to the audiovisual experience. A large, square space was transformed into a home cinema and music room, fitted with top-quality speakers, amplifiers, projector, and film screen. The walls were acoustically designed with one-directional diffusers in wood and with heavy drapes that aid in absorbing sound and creating the optimal conditions for viewing and listening.

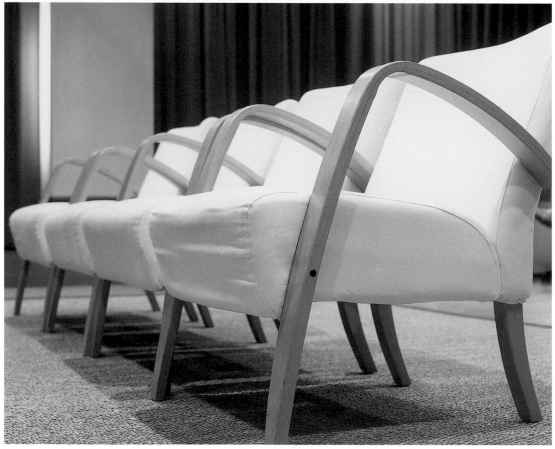

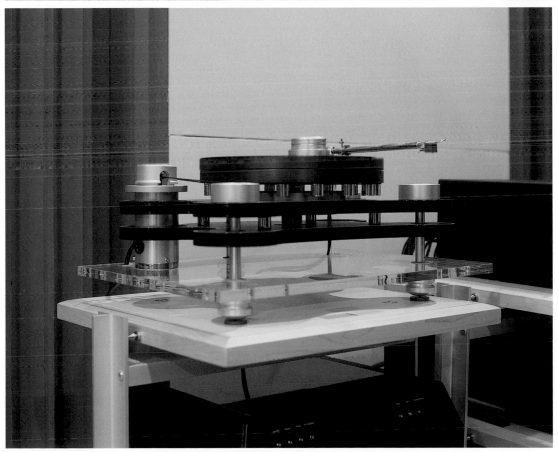

Room with a View

Architect: **Pamela Furze**
Location: **London, UK**
Photos © **Ken Hayden/**
Redcover.com

Designed by Pamela Furze for her husband David and herself, this master bedroom integrates a home cinema into the wall, complete with built-in speakers. The projector is built into a partition that divides the bed from the closets behind, concealing the electrical installations and situating the projector at the correct height for the most comfortable viewing position. Certainly nothing beats watching movies in the comfort of your own bed.

Jose Maria Santos House

Architect: **Pont Reyes**

Location: **Barcelona, Spain**

Photos © **Gogortza/Llorella**

A partition made of wood panels was designed to accommodate a large panoramic screen, doubling as a spatial divider in this Barcelona flat. High-definition speakers were placed above the screen, and the images are projected from a projector hung from the living-room ceiling. Situated next to a terrace, special shutters were installed to isolate the space from daylight and ensure the best viewing conditions.

Time-Out

Unwind in the comfort of your own home: Game rooms, indoor pools, private gyms, and more

Bachelor's Game Room

Architect: **Cortney and Robert Novogratz**
Location: **New York, NY, USA**
Photos © **Joshua McHugh**

Forming part of the previously featured Manhattan bachelor pad, this game room features a 1941 Brunswick pool table and a side table on which to play board games or from which to enjoy watching a round of pool. A sleek, contemporary aesthetic is provided by the roughly painted walls, dark wood floors, unique light fixtures, and combination of styles. The photographs of Tupac and Easy E were taken by Chi Modu.

House in Rome

Architect: **Patrizio Romano Paris**
Location: **Rome, Italy**
Photos © **Reto Guntli/Zapaimages**

A spacious room linked to the main living area through an open portico houses a modern billiard room in this residence in Rome. An elegant billiard table is flanked by velvet flower stools in vivid shades of blue and lilac, matched by an unusual lamp that hangs overhead. The carefully designed lighting system aims to provide both direct and indirect light to create a dramatic and theatrical effect.

Pool Attic

Design: **Peter Pallai**
Location: **Brighton, UK**
Photos © **Ed Reeve/Redcover.com**

The upper level of a two-story home was converted into an entertainment area with a pool table that takes center stage. The space also features a chill-out corner and a stepladder leading to a small platform sustained by wooden beams. This serves as a resting area with a unique bird's-eye view of the game. Industrial metal sheets were placed underneath the heavy objects to avoid damaging the parquet floors.

Playroom

Architect: **Nico Rensch**

Location: **London, UK**

Photos © **Mark Luscombe-Whyte/ The Interior Archive**

A pool table, percussion set, and large poufs compose this adult playroom, which offers a variety of activities for the owners and their guests to enjoy during their leisure time. The drums are placed on a circular pedestal to add a theatrical quality and allow the player to feel as if on a stage set. A large shelf unit on the wall emphasizes the playful character of the rooms and provides space for decorative objects.

Summer House

Design: **Owners**
Location: **Barcelona, Spain**
Photos © **Gogortza/Llorella**

Located in the outskirts of Barcelona, this house is used as a family vacation home for special holidays and the summer months. Inherited by the sons of an avid hunter, the house contains a game room that features a billiard table, set within a lavishly designed interior. The space was also conceived as a "trophy room," exhibiting the extensive collection of hunting trophies obtained by the father of the family more than thirty years ago.

Industrial House

Design: **Mark Mack Architecture**

Location: **Venice, CA, USA**

Photos © **Undine Pröhl**

This project consists of a typical adaptation of the traditional artist's loft, with large, open spaces than can be used for both living and working purposes. One of the areas on the ground floor is designated as a playroom in which to play Ping-Pong. Given its spacious character and industrial quality, it can be used as an indoor playroom for children without worrying too much about damaging the floor or furniture.

Switalski House

Architect: **John Corrigan**

Location: **Surrey, UK**

Photos © **Johnny Bouchier/**

Redcover.com

Located in the city of Wentworth, in Surrey, this house incorporates a foosball table in the living room area, next to the glass doors that lead out to the garden. The table provides a fun activity for youngsters after school and on weekends, as well as for adults during gatherings or dinner parties. It also serves as another element of the interior design, integrating with the neutral palette of the floor and furnishings.

Country House

Location: **Salisbury, UK**

Photos © **Martyn O'Kelly/**
Redcover.com

Billiard rooms are most often characterized by a traditional design consisting of antique furnishings, dark wood, and subdued colors. This room exemplifies the typical style of a classic billiard room, surrounded by a traditional décor and restrained palette. Details like the green lamps above the table and benches upholstered in plaid aid in creating an authentic atmosphere for playing pool at home.

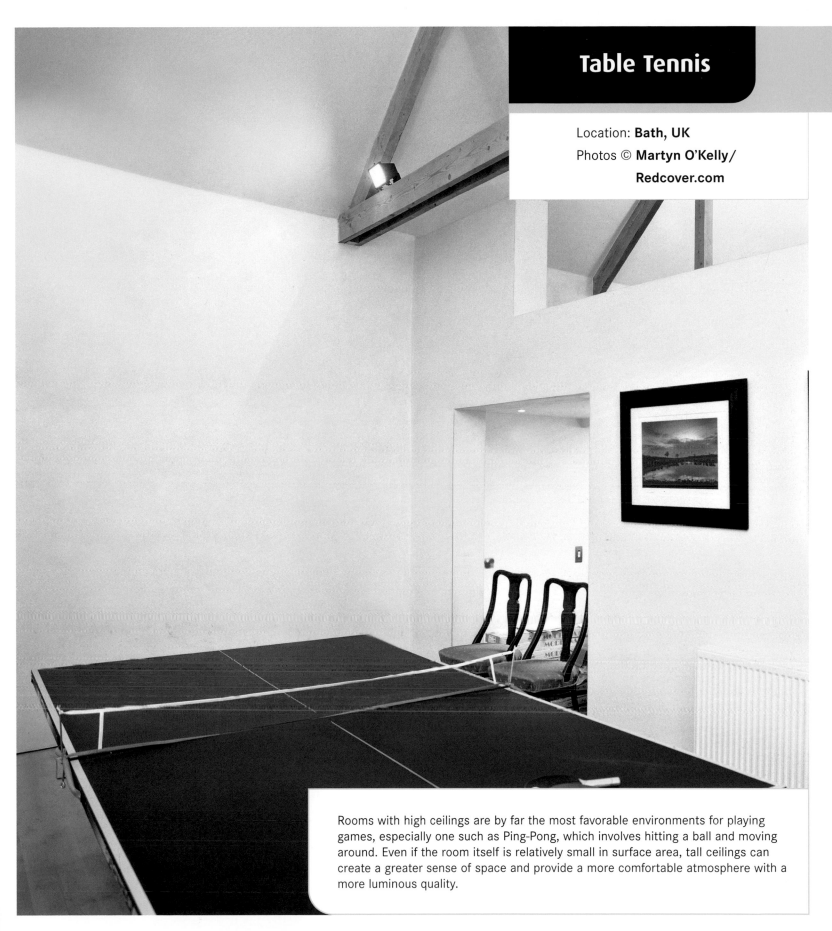

Table Tennis

Location: **Bath, UK**
Photos © **Martyn O'Kelly/**
Redcover.com

Rooms with high ceilings are by far the most favorable environments for playing games, especially one such as Ping-Pong, which involves hitting a ball and moving around. Even if the room itself is relatively small in surface area, tall ceilings can create a greater sense of space and provide a more comfortable atmosphere with a more luminous quality.

Brock House

Architect: **Roderick James Architects**

Location: **Berkshire, UK**

Photos © **Anthony Harrison/**

Redcover.com

A large room situated at the corner of a house was designed as a child's playroom, creating a specific area in which to keep toys and other playthings. If space is not an issue, the inclusion of a foosball table can be especially convenient and entertaining for both children and adults. Creating a separate playroom can also serve to keep children's rooms more tidy and less cluttered.

Hermitage House

Design: **Artcoustic (speakers)**
Location: **London, UK**
Photos © **Artcoustic**

The top floor of a London home was turned into a game and media room, featuring a modern billiard table, a large projection screen, and sophisticated audio equipment. The speakers, designed by Artcoustic, are concealed behind the screen, while the projector is kept out of sight within a side table. Low furnishings and large poufs emphasize the casual atmosphere of space, designed as a leisure room for adults.

Hampstead House

Design: **Artcoustic (speakers)**
Location: **London, UK**
Photos © **Artcoustic**

As an updated version of the classic poolroom, this space integrates a pool table into a modern home through the use of contemporary furnishings and light fixtures while also incorporating a sleek and discreet audio system designed by Artcoustic. Comfortable armchairs and an overall neutral design generate a laid-back atmosphere in which owners and guests can enjoy playing pool while listening to music through high-quality loudspeakers.

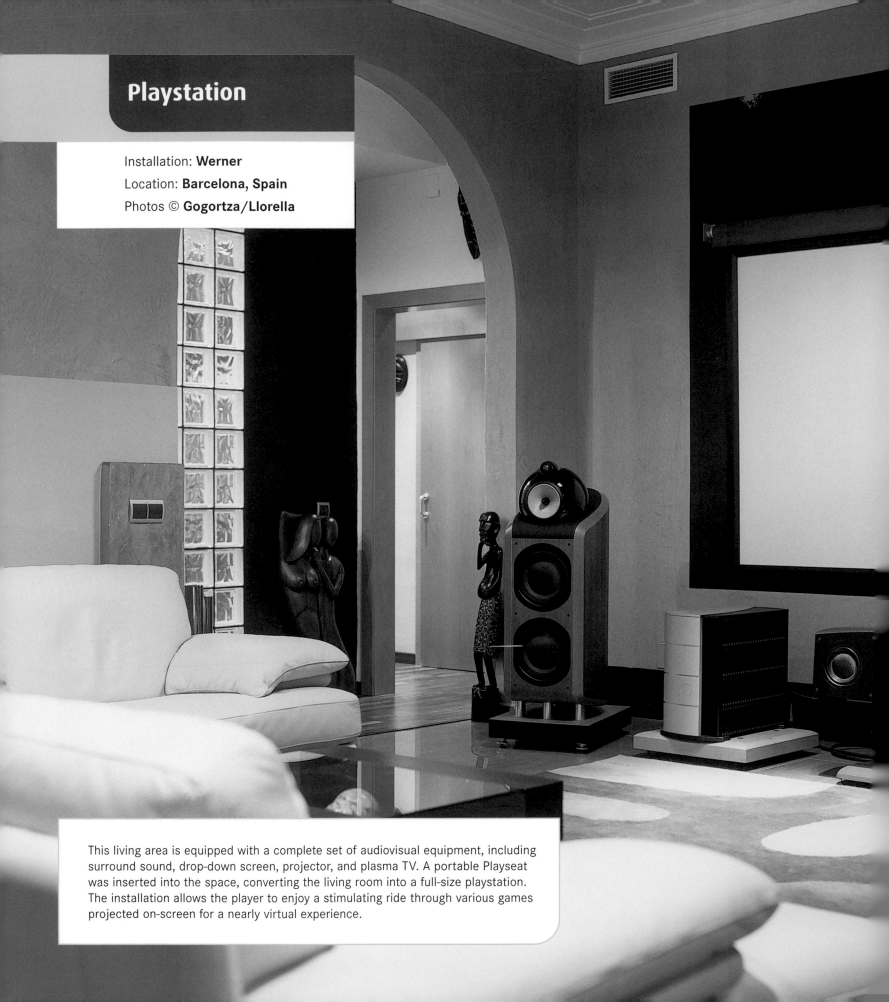

Playstation

Installation: **Werner**
Location: **Barcelona, Spain**
Photos © **Gogortza/Llorella**

This living area is equipped with a complete set of audiovisual equipment, including surround sound, drop-down screen, projector, and plasma TV. A portable Playseat was inserted into the space, converting the living room into a full-size playstation. The installation allows the player to enjoy a stimulating ride through various games projected on-screen for a nearly virtual experience.

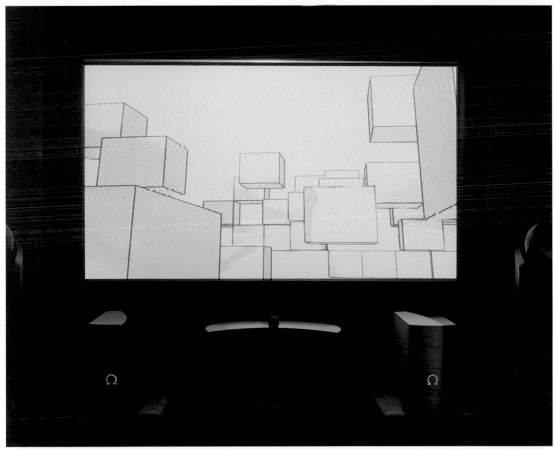

Slice House

Design: **Proctor: Rihl**
Location: **Porto Alegre, Brazil**
Photos © **Marcelo Nunes**

This swimming pool, not quite indoor given that its access is situated on an exterior balcony, was conceived as a visual element to provide a voyeuristic experience for those within the home. The glass structure, supported by the side walls, was integrated into the living area to serve as a daylight filter, creating rippled water effects during the day, and as an oversized light fixture at night. The visual spectacle offers a unique experience not often attributed to private swimming pools.

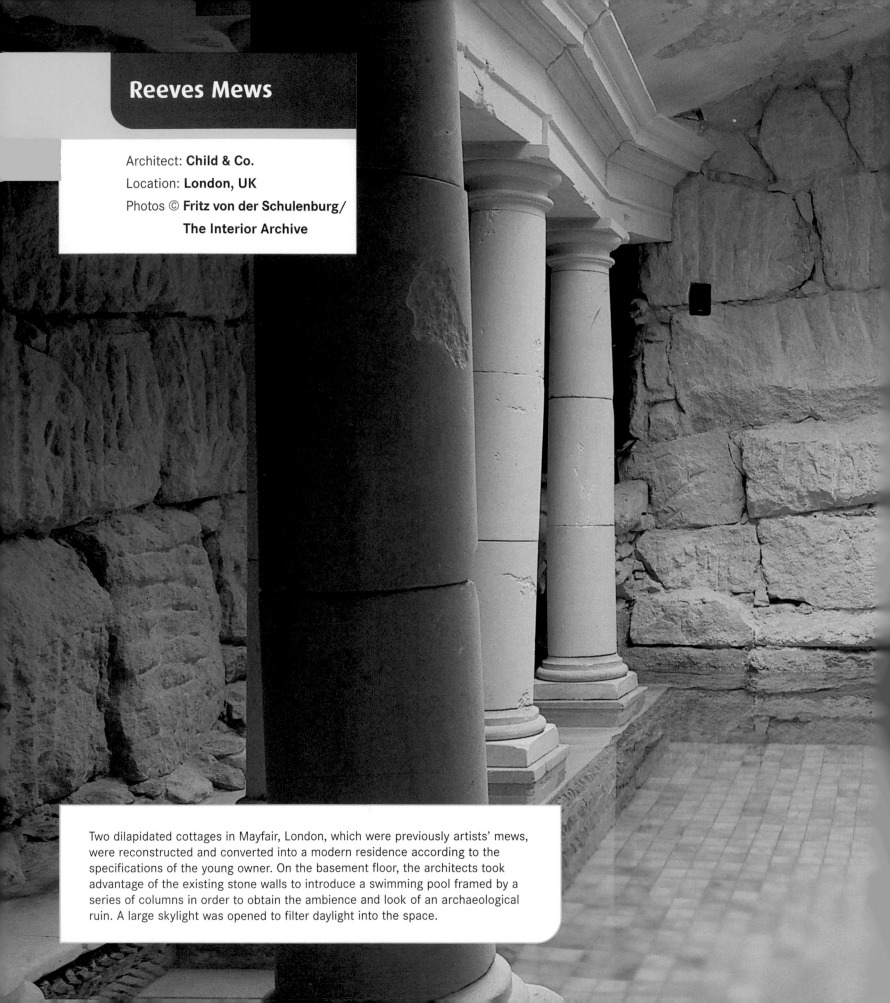

Reeves Mews

Architect: **Child & Co.**
Location: **London, UK**
Photos © **Fritz von der Schulenburg/ The Interior Archive**

Two dilapidated cottages in Mayfair, London, which were previously artists' mews, were reconstructed and converted into a modern residence according to the specifications of the young owner. On the basement floor, the architects took advantage of the existing stone walls to introduce a swimming pool framed by a series of columns in order to obtain the ambience and look of an archaeological ruin. A large skylight was opened to filter daylight into the space.

Indoor Pool

Architect: **Paxton Locher**
Location: **London, UK**
Photos © **Luke White/The Interior Archive**

An indoor pool is often synonymous with luxury, given both the spatial and economical requirements that such an installation entails. This spectacular indoor pool, occupying the central area of a 4,000 square foot residence, enjoys the light and views provided by the double-height space in which it is situated. Its open character and integration into the living areas allow for animated interaction between those inside the pool and those inside the adjoining living space.

Pool and Slide

Design: **Artcoustic (speakers)**

Location: **London, UK**

Photos © **Artcoustic**

Functioning as an entertainment room in more ways than one, this interior, which features a wide-screen TV and speakers designed by Artcoustic, incorporates a large swimming pool with its own spiral slide. The slide structure, which can be accessed by way of an upper mezzanine level, was suspended from the ceiling in order not to obstruct the surrounding pool area. Swimmers can enjoy a dip in the pool to the sound of music or sit and enjoy videos or movies.

Sheldon Avenue

Architect: **Belsize Architects**
Location: **London, UK**
Photos © **Graham Atkins/**
Redcover.com

Indoor pools are always considered a fun part of the house, given their unique interior setting and the fact that they can be used at any time throughout the year. This basement pool structure, partially wrapped in glass and visible from the house's garden, is visually linked to the upper floor by way of a large sheet of structural glass in the floor of the entrance area that looks through to the swimming pool beneath.

Oval Room and Pool

Architect: **Wood/Marsh Architecture**
Location: **Victoria, Australia**
Photos © **Trevor Mein_meinphoto**

This leisure space forms part of the conversion of the top level of an existing three-story warehouse located in a semi-industrial precinct in Prahran. The dilapidated former sweatshop was converted into a family home for a couple and their three sons, inserting sculptural forms like this oval room that reinterpret and create new forms of living. The room serves as a comfortable and unexpected chill-out space, ideal for relaxing after a swim in the large pool lit in red, which creates a dramatic, theatrical effect.

Private House

Architect: **Formwork Architects**
Location: **London, UK**
Photos © **Dennis Gilbert/VIEW**

Finding a place inside the home for a private gym is not always the easiest task, especially if space is an issue and there are no extra rooms in which to conceal the often unattractive equipment. The architects of this private home designated the car garage as the gym room, combining the two functions by way of a platform lift that accommodates the machines when lowered and, when elevated, makes room for the family car.

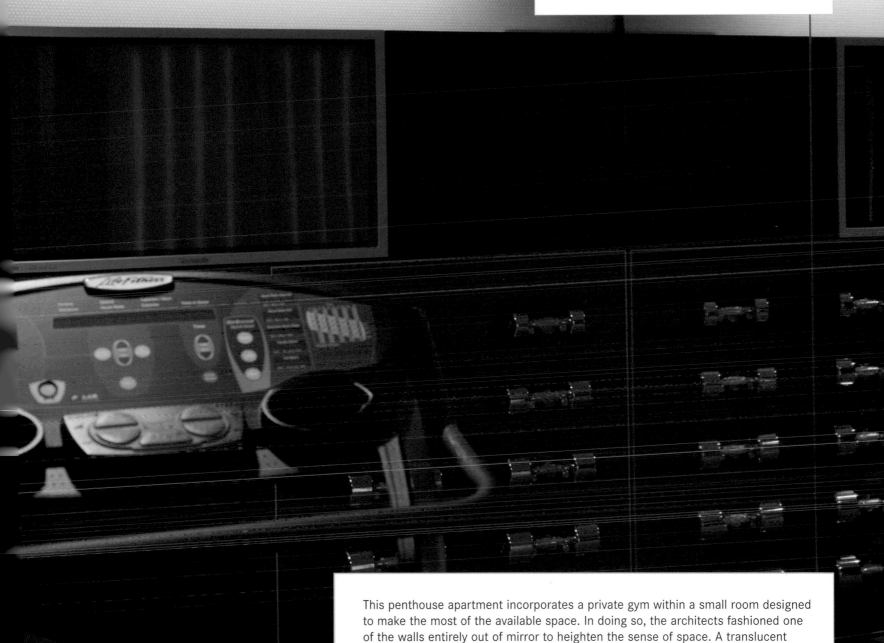

Wharf Apartment

Design: **Alison Brooks Architects**
Location: **London, UK**
Photos © **Dennis Gilbert/VIEW**

This penthouse apartment incorporates a private gym within a small room designed to make the most of the available space. In doing so, the architects fashioned one of the walls entirely out of mirror to heighten the sense of space. A translucent material was used to create a clerestory window that, when lit from behind, provides a pleasant, diffused glow within the room. The wall is equipped with various machines and wall-hung weights, while a flat-screen TV offers the opportunity to combine exercise and entertainment.

VXO House

Architect: **Alison Brooks Architects**
Location: **London, UK**
Photos © **Mark York/Redcover.com**

Composed of three individual structures that integrate landscape, structural form, and art into a visual and spatial narrative, the VXO House incorporates an X-Pavilion that serves as a private gym and guesthouse. A vertical timber wall screens a shower room, audiovisual cabinet, and storage room. Enveloped in glass walls, the space becomes the perfect place in which to exercise, meditate, or simply contemplate the views of the surrounding greenery.

Binny & Graham House

Location: **Sussex, UK**

Photos © **Christopher Drake/ Redcover.com**

A Ping-Pong table brings out the kid in most adults, being one of the classic table games of all time. Its portable and compact nature make it the perfect game for keeping at home, regardless of whether space is available to create a room especially designated to entertainment. Practically any living area can be transformed into a fun room by introducing a Ping-Pong table, which can be easily folded and stored away when not in use.

Gym and AV Studio

Design: **Owner and Gibson Music Ltd.**
Location: **London, UK**
Photos © **Fritz von der Schulenburg/ The Interior Archive**

A large room within a London flat was designed to accommodate a private gym and media room in one. The gym, equipped with a complete weight machine next to a mirrored wall, is situated next to an audiovisual presentation suite with multi-source audio and graphics developed by Gibson Music. A sitting area allows tenants and guests to enjoy a quiet rest after a workout or to savor an entertaining session with visual and sound stimulation.

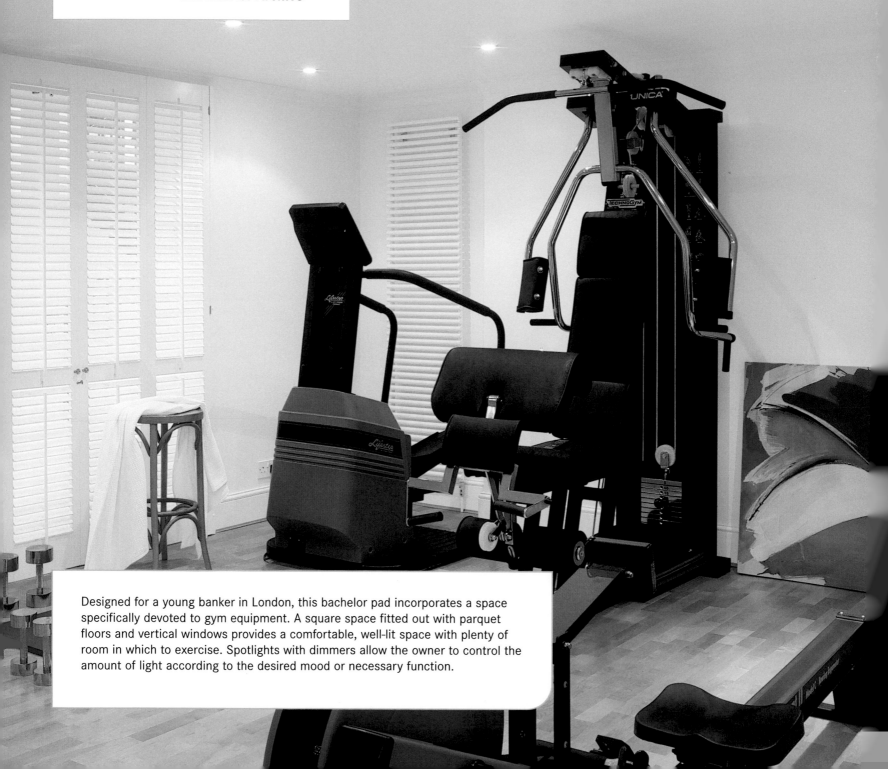

Bachelor Pad

Interior design: **Dina Lamberton**
Location: **London, UK**
Photos © **Fritz von der Schulenburg/ The Interior Archive**

Designed for a young banker in London, this bachelor pad incorporates a space specifically devoted to gym equipment. A square space fitted out with parquet floors and vertical windows provides a comfortable, well-lit space with plenty of room in which to exercise. Spotlights with dimmers allow the owner to control the amount of light according to the desired mood or necessary function.

Home Gym with Screen

Architect: **Ajrapetov**
Location: **Moscow, Russia**
Photos © **Fritz von der Schulenburg/ The Interior Archive**

This apartment in Moscow includes a large private gym with views toward the city. The space features a complete set of exercise equipment and machines, along with its very own tanning bed. A pivoting plasma screen hung from the ceiling provides simultaneous visual entertainment, and beyond a pair of glass doors, a sauna offers a relaxing postworkout treatment.

Play It by Ear

Music to your ears: Rooms for playing and listening

House S

Architect: **Oskar Leo Kaufman**
Location: **Bezau, Austria**
Photos © **Adolf Bereuter**

Located in a small Austrian town, this house incorporates a sound studio on the basement floor. Situated belowground to contain noise levels, the room is provided with natural light by way of a skylight in an adjacent space. Enclosed within a single open area containing a stepped level, the room features a glass wall that allows light in from the adjoining space and undulating walls designed to evenly distribute sound. The walls are also soundproofed to isolate the noise from the remaining areas of the home.

House in Highgate

Architect: **Eldridge Smerin**

Location: **London, UK**

Photos © **Chris Gascoigne/VIEW**

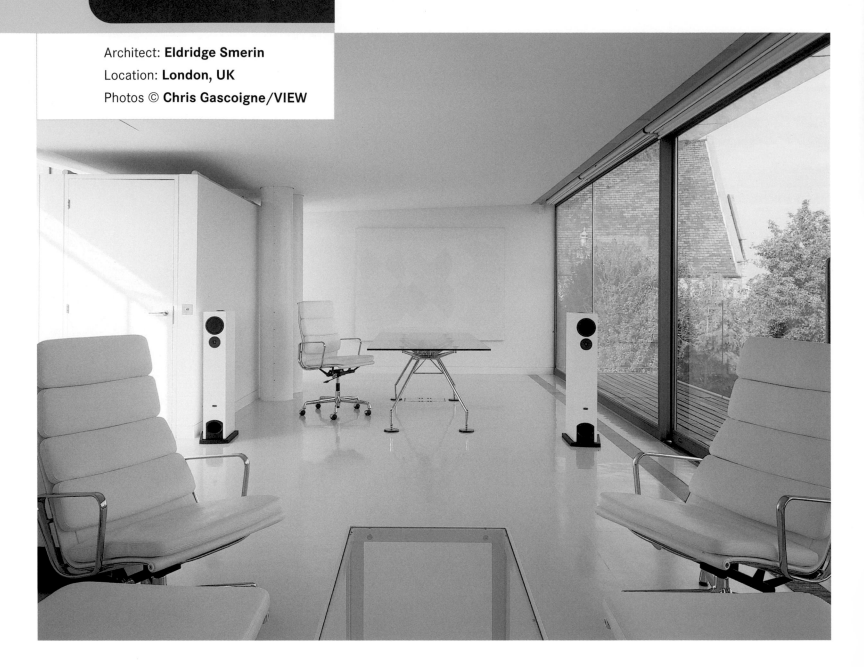

A meeting area on the upper level of this house in Highgate was designed as an office area with an incorporated sound system that provides listening entertainment to clients, guests, and owners alike. The comfortable contemporary furniture and white interiors create a futuristic effect complemented by the modern loudspeakers, which are used as freestanding elements and also integrated into a wall unit.

Seating Pods

Architect: **Darren Gander**

Location: **London, UK**

Photos © **Luke White/The Interior Archive**

Set against a neutral backdrop, a pair of plastic modular chairs, funky lamps, and a matching red table and rug create the perfect setting for chilling out and listening to music. Two record decks and a bubble speaker allow the tenants to sit back and enjoy tunes, out loud or through headphones, while contemplating the colorful designs and cool atmosphere.

Q-Loft

Architect: **Resolution: 4 Architecture**

Location: **New York, NY, USA**

Photos © **Floto + Warner**

Forming part of the Q-Loft designed for the Marvel Comics editor in chief, this artist's studio also accommodates a set of musical instruments and the owner's extensive collection of comic artifacts. The playful character of the space is emphasized by the installation of numerous built-in shelves made of acrylic that are internally lit for a dramatic and dynamic effect.

Jones House

Design: **Artcoustic (speakers)**
Location: **London, UK**
Photos © **Artcoustic**

This living room boasts Artcoustic's cutting-edge audio system, which integrates high-quality acoustics with artistic design. The loudspeaker frames can be tailor-made to complement any interior, providing a choice from a wide range of textile designs created by handpicked artists from around the world. These textiles transform the speakers into hanging works of art that can be contemplated while listening to music. In this case, the owner preferred to leave the speakers uncovered, lending a high-tech aesthetic to the room.

Audio Tower

Architect: **Ajrapetov**

Location: **Moscow, Russia**

Photos © **Fritz von der Schulenburg/ The Interior Archive**

Situated within a loft, this residence accommodates an open-plan living area with several leisure areas. A sitting area adjacent to the main living room features a vertical audiovisual unit and telescope with which to contemplate the stars at night. The tower houses a fully equipped sound installation that offers a pleasurable listening experience in the comfort of leather lounge chairs with views toward the terrace.

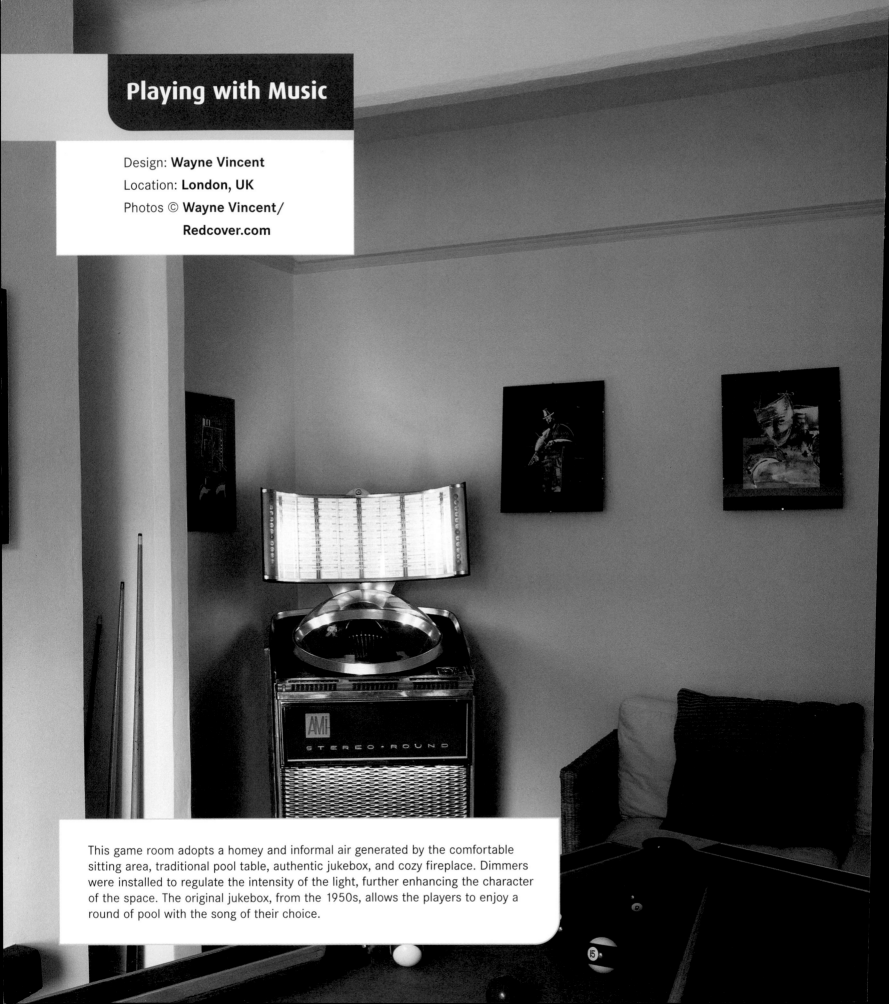

Playing with Music

Design: **Wayne Vincent**
Location: **London, UK**
Photos © **Wayne Vincent/**
Redcover.com

This game room adopts a homey and informal air generated by the comfortable sitting area, traditional pool table, authentic jukebox, and cozy fireplace. Dimmers were installed to regulate the intensity of the light, further enhancing the character of the space. The original jukebox, from the 1950s, allows the players to enjoy a round of pool with the song of their choice.

Dunbar Residence

Architect: **Nick Milkovich and Arthur Erickson**

Location: **Maui, HI, USA**

Photos © **Ron Dahlquist**

This oceanfront house in Hawaii belongs to a former music producer who entrusted the design to architects Nick Milkovich and Arthur Erickson. The layout of the new house was to include a room devoted to music where the owner could display his record collection and indulge his passion for percussion with family and friends. Located on the first floor, the room is soundproofed to the highest professional standards in order to isolate noise from the surrounding areas of the home.

Piano Room

Architect: Owners
Location: **London, UK**
Photos © **Johnny Bouchier/
Redcover.com**

Set within a typical London flat, this grand piano was placed in a corner of the living room next to the fireplace. A piano, as pleasurable to play as to listen to, is one of the most seductive instruments when it comes to entertaining guests, family, and friends. Not only a feast for the ears, the piano can also be a feast for the eyes, instantly lending a sophisticated character to the interior design.

Clayton House

Architect: **ADP Architects**
Location: **London, UK**
Photos © **Alex Ramsey/**
Redcover.com

This attic space was conceived as a music room, taking advantage of the area underneath the sloping ceiling to place an electric piano and an adjacent sitting area. The simplicity of the room demonstrates how easy it can be to achieve an attractive entertainment room with few resources, and how to get the most out of the more awkward spaces within the home.

FUNiture
&
Things

Playful furniture
and fun accessories

Manhattan Apartment

Interior design: **Karim Rashid**
Location: **New York, NY, USA**
Photos © **Simon Upton/The Interior Archive**

Karim Rashid's studio apartment in Manhattan can be considered a fun room as a whole, given the vivid and dynamic character of the furnishings that decorate the interior. Plush poufs, velvety textures, and curved forms are combined with 1960s and 1970s patterns and bright colors to create a lighthearted atmosphere that is visually entertaining for all the senses. The designer constantly renews the décor so that the pieces in his apartment are never more than five years old.

Retro Penthouse

Architect: **1100 Architect**
Interior designer: **Tony Ingrao**
Location: **New York, NY, USA**
Photos © **Reto Guntli/Zapaimages**

For the apartment owner's daughter, interior designer Tony Ingrao created a bedroom inspired by Barbie's bedroom circa 1970. A playful atmosphere is provided by the vivid pink shades used for both the walls and the furnishings, as well as by the contrast of unusual textures and light fixtures. The ottomans, covered in plastic and suede, glow when sat upon; the vintage sofa is covered in double-knit wool.

Private Apartment

Owner: **Darren Gander**
Location: **London, UK**
Photos © **Luke White/The Interior Archive**

The dining area of a contemporary residence need not be reserved or minimal to express elegance. A subtle mixture of styles, forms, and materials in adequate measures can achieve a fun and sophisticated design such as this one, which includes a 1960s-inspired white plastic table and bucket PVC chairs, in addition to a freestanding fish tank that provides a visual treat for the onlookers. Colorful and funky light fixtures add life to this room as well, which can also serve as a space in which to play games at leisure.

Bobo House

Interior design: **Cristina Rodríguez**
Location: **Barcelona, Spain**
Photos © **Jordi Sarrà**

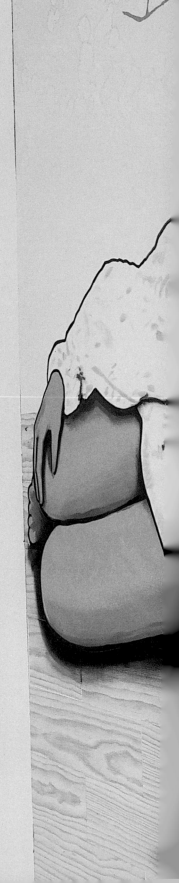

Kids' rooms can also be stylishly fun. In this house in Barcelona, the entrance to the child's playroom is decorated with a hand-painted mural, while the furnishings and light fixtures are contemporary in style. A thoughtful arrangement of different elements and the presence of furnishings such as the chalkboard bench exhibit imaginative touches that bring out the fun side of practical objects.

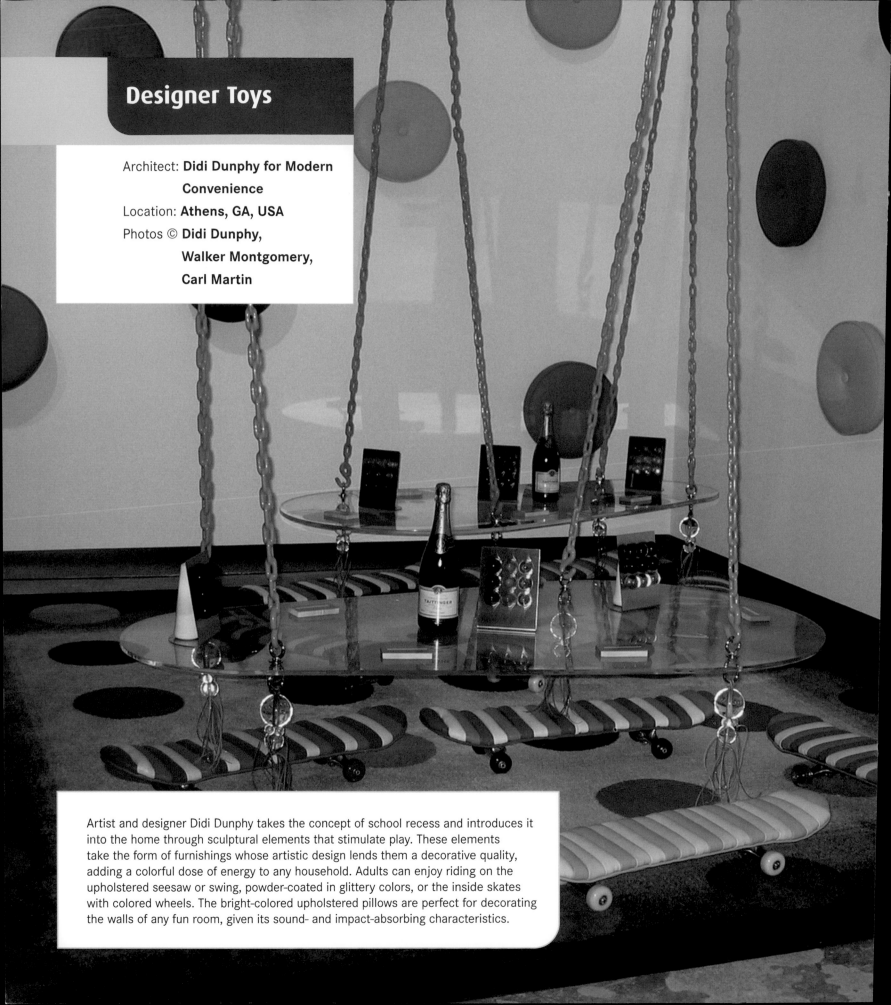

Designer Toys

Architect: **Didi Dunphy for Modern Convenience**
Location: **Athens, GA, USA**
Photos © **Didi Dunphy, Walker Montgomery, Carl Martin**

Artist and designer Didi Dunphy takes the concept of school recess and introduces it into the home through sculptural elements that stimulate play. These elements take the form of furnishings whose artistic design lends them a decorative quality, adding a colorful dose of energy to any household. Adults can enjoy riding on the upholstered seesaw or swing, powder-coated in glittery colors, or the inside skates with colored wheels. The bright-colored upholstered pillows are perfect for decorating the walls of any fun room, given its sound- and impact-absorbing characteristics.

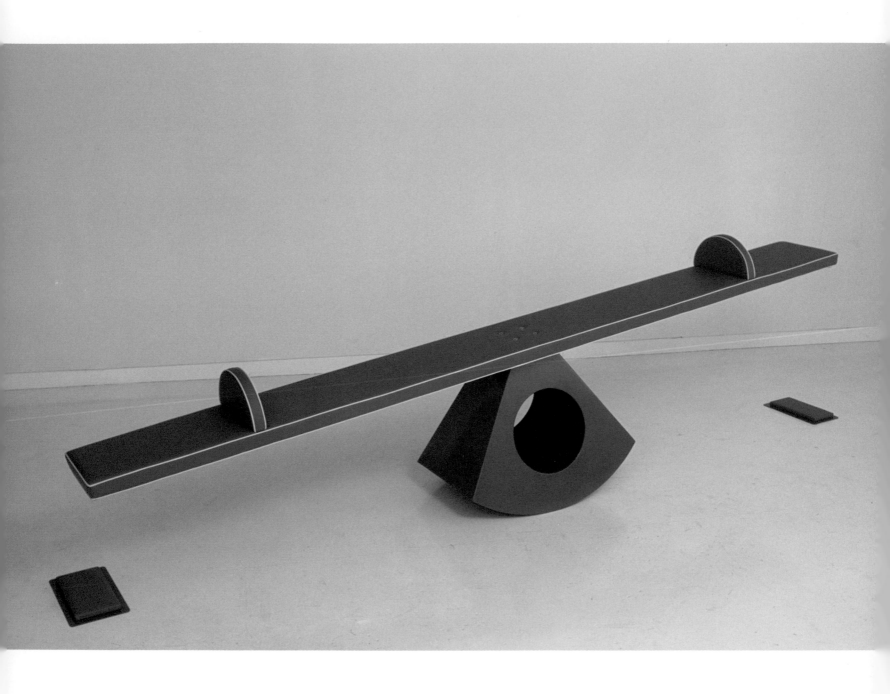

Artcoustic

Architect: **Artcoustic**

Location: **Copenhagen, Denmark**

Photos © **Artcoustic**

Founded by a Scandinavian couple with a passion for sound and art, the Artcoustic technology combines the aesthetic lure of artistic design with the quality and precision of state-of-the-art audio equipment. The loudspeakers, which occupy the depth of an average picture frame, feature interchangeable screens that can be printed with a range of exclusive artworks to match the interior décor. Unlike other flat speakers, this dynamic collection employs a system that enables a superior frequency response to monitors with more than twice the internal volume, delivering what would normally be associated with studio-quality monitoring.

FUN ROOMS—Sources

LIGHTS OUT

Many companies offer home theater systems, which may include televisions with LCD (liquid crystal display) or plasma screens, projection televisions and projectors, and high-end audio systems. A few of the industry leaders are:

Canon
One Canon Plaza
Lake Success, NY 11042-1198
Phone: 1-516-328-5000
www.usa.canon.com

Hewlett-Packard
3000 Hanover Street
Palo Alto, CA 94304-1185
Phone: 1-650-857-1501
www.hp.com

InFocus
27700B SW Parkway Avenue
Wilsonville, OR 97070-9215
Phone: 1-503-685-8888
Toll-Free: 1-800-294-6400
www.infocus.com

Panasonic
One Panasonic Way
Secaucus, NJ 07094
Phone: 1-201-348-7000
www.panasonic.com

Philips Electronics
64 Perimeter Center East
Atlanta, GA 30346
Phone: 1-770-821-2400
www.philipsusa.com

Pioneer Electronics
2265 East 220th Street
Long Beach, CA 90810
Toll-Free: 1-800-746-6337
www.pioneerelectronics.com

Samsung Electronics
105 Challenger Road
Ridgefield Park, NJ 07660
Phone: 1-800-SAMSUNG
www.samsung.com

Sony
550 Madison Avenue
New York, NY 10022
Phone: 1-212-833-6800
www.sony.com

TIME-OUT

Relaxation centers often feature game-centered activities such as a billiard, ping-pong, or foosball tables. They may also include indoor pools and private gyms.

Billiards

A comprehensive listing of billiard manufacturers can be found at www.billiardsdigest.com/bd_megamall. Some notable companies include:

AMF Billiards & Games
106 Lyford Street
Bland, MO 65014
Toll-Free: 1-800-325-0087
www.amfbilliards.com

Brunswick Billiards
8663 196th Avenue
Bristol, WI 53104
Phone: 1-262-857-7374
Toll-Free: 1-800-336-8764
www.brunswick-billiards.com

Diamond Billiard Products
4700 New Middle Road
Jeffersonville, IN 47130
Phone: 1-812-288-7665
www.diamondbilliardproducts.com

Olhausen Billiards
12460 Kirkham Court
Poway, CA 92064
Phone: 1-858-486-0761
www.olhausenbilliards.com

ProLine Billiard
3601 S. Sanford Avenue
Sanford, FL 32773
Phone: 1-407-324-4171
www.prolinebilliard.com

Steepleton
927 E. Broadway
Louisville, KY 40204
Phone: 1-502-585-2396
www.steepleton.com
Ping-Pong

A wide selection of table tennis manufacturers can be found at www.ping-pong.com. Some highlights include:

Butterfly
4482 Technology Drive
Wilson, NC 27896
Phone: 1-252-291-4770
Toll-Free: 1-800-611-7712
www.butterflyonline.com

Harvard
c/o Escalade Sports
P.O. Box 889
Evansville, IN 47706
Phone: 1-812-467-1200
www.escaladesports.com

Kettler
P.O. Box 2747
Virginia Beach, VA 23450-2747
Phone: 1-757-427-2400
www.kettlerusa.com

Prince
c/o DMI Sports Source
375 Commerce Drive
Fort Washington, PA 19034
Phone: 1-215-283-0153
Toll-Free: 1-800-423-3220
www.dmisports.com

Stiga
c/o Escalade Sports
P.O. Box 889
Evansville, IN 47706
Phone: 1-812-467-1200
www.escaladesports.com
www.tabletennis.se

Foosball

For information on foosball, check www.foosball.com. Notable manufacturers of foosball tables include:

Bonzini USA
282 Knollcrest Drive
Pinnacle, NC 27043
Phone: 1-336-325-3183
www.bonziniusa.com

Carrom
P.O. Box 649
Ludington, MI 49431
Phone: 1-231-845-1263
www.carrom.com

Rock-it
Uptrend Industries Ltd.
1927 Boblett Street
Blaine, WA 98230
Phone: 1-604-961-1698
Toll-Free: 1-800-770-4263
www.tablesoccer.com

Shelti
333 Morton Street
Bay City, MI 48706
Phone: 1-989-893-1739
www.shelti.com

Tornado
P.O. Box 637
Summerfield, NC 27358
Phone: 1-336-210 -1194
www.tornadofoosball.com

Indoor Pools

Many different kinds of indoor pools are available, including those that feature water-resist technology. A few notable manufacturers are:

Endless Pools
200 East Dutton Mill Road
Aston, PA 19014
Phone: 1-610-497-8676
Toll-Free: 1-800-732-8660
www.endlesspools.com

SwimEx
846 Airport Road
Fall River, MA 02720
Phone: 1-508-646-1600
Toll-Free: 1-800-877-7946
www.swimex.com

Gyms

The Sporting Goods Manufacturers Association has a useful website at www.sgma.com. A few companies that specialize in equipment for the home are listed below.

Bowflex
1400 NE 136th Avenue
Vancouver, WA 98684
Toll-Free: 1-800-BOWFLEX
www.bowflex.com

Life Fitness
5100 N. River Road
Schiller Park, IL 60176
Toll-Free: 1-800-351-3737
www.lifefitness.com

Nautilus
1400 NE 136th Avenue
Vancouver, WA 98684
Toll-Free: 1-800-782-4799
www.nautilus.com

Soloflex
570 NE 53rd Avenue
Hillsboro, OR 97124
Toll-Free: 1-800-547-8802
www.soloflex.com

Total Gym
7755 Arjons Drive
San Diego, CA 92126
Toll-Free: 1-800-541-4900
www.totalgym.com

Play it by Ear

Your ideal fun room might be a music studio, a living area with a fully equipped sound system, or a high-tech environment to play video games. Here is a selection of high-end manufacturers of audio systems and accessories:

Artcoustic
c/o St. John Group
4396 Saddlestone Drive
Bellingham, WA 98226
Phone: 1-360-756-2205
www.artcoustic.com

Bose
Mountain Road
Framingham, MA 01701
Toll-Free: 1-800-WWW-BOSE
www.bose.com

Bowers & Wilkins
Dale Road
Worthing
BN11 2BH West Sussex
UK
Phone: 011-44-1903-221-800
www.bwspeakers.com

Unit 8
50 Sulivan Road
SW6 3DX London UK
Phone: 011-44-20-7384-2270
www.gibson-music.com

Krell
45 Connair Road
Orange, CT 06477-3650
Phone: 1-203-799-9954
www.krellonline.com

Playseats
16625 Redmond Way, Suite 204
Redmond, MA 98052
Phone: 425-861-9100
www.playseatsusa.biz

Sony
550 Madison Avenue
New York, NY 10022
Phone: 1-212-833-6800
www.sony.com

Yamaha
6660 Orangethorpe Avenue
Buena Park, CA 90620
Phone: 1-714-522-9105
www.yamaha.com

FURNITURE & THINGS

Selecting furniture for your fun room is a highly personal process. A number of innovative designers create playful accessories, including:

Blu Dot
3236 California Street NE
Minneapolis, MN 55418
Phone: 1-612-782-1844
www.bludot.com

Cappellini Design
22060 Arosio (CO)
Italy
Phone: 011-39-031-759111
www.cappellini.it
Dakota Jackson

D&D Building, Suite 407
979 Third Avenue
New York, NY 10022
Phone: 1-212-838-9444
www.dakotajackson.com

Didi Dunphy, Designer
Modern Convenience
421 Dearing Street
Athens, GA 30605
Phone: 1-706-208-8242
www.modernconvenience.com

Karim Rashid
357 West 17th Street
New York, NY 10011
Phone: 1-212-929-8657
www.karimrashid.com

Karim Rashid Shop
137 West 19th Street
New York, NY 10011
Phone: 1-212-337 8078
www.karimrashidshop.com

Skypad Furniture
296 King Street East
Toronto, Ontario
M5A 1K4
Canada
Phone: 1-416-762-8129
www.skypadfurniture.com

Tony Ingrao
Ingrao, Inc.
17 East 64th Street
New York, NY 10021
Phone: 1-212-472-5400

The Terence Conran Shop
Bridgemarket
407 East 59th Street
New York, NY 10022
Phone: 1-212-755-9079
www.conran.com/shop